THE
Archive Photographs
SERIES
MALMESBURY

Daniel's Well,   Malmesbury.

MALMESBVRY

Upper High Street,   Malmesbury.

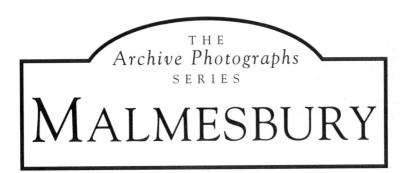

THE
Archive Photographs
SERIES

MALMESBURY

Compiled by
Dorothy Barnes

CHALFORD

First published 1995
Copyright © Author names, 1995

The Chalford Publishing Company
St Mary's Mill, Chalford,
Stroud, Gloucestershire, GL6 8NX

ISBN 0 7524 0177 7

Typesetting and origination by
The Chalford Publishing Company
Printed in Great Britain by
Redwood Books, Trowbridge

Market Cross, Malmesbury

Contents

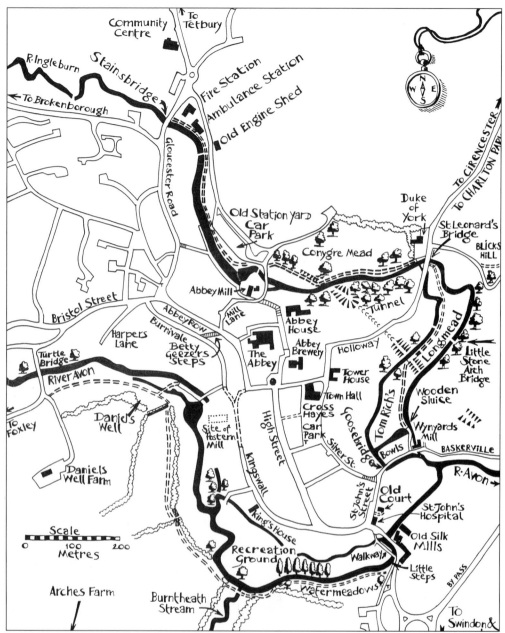

Map of Malmesbury (drawn by Tristram Forward).

Introduction

I have realised for a number of years that we are living in an era of rapidly changing times.

While there are many very interesting books on the factual history of Malmesbury, very few reveal the conditions of life of the average person during the Victorian period and really to the end of the First World War. From then onwards, with the introduction of electricity, motor vehicles, and aircraft, the standard of living showed marked changes.

My late parents, Edward and Elizabeth Barnes, were unitedly adamant that the days of their youth were 'The Good Old Days'. This I strongly opposed, pointing out the poverty, hardships and suffering endured. I was told in no uncertain tones, that as I wasn't alive then, I was in no position to argue on the subject.

However, after their demise, I started the thankless task of sorting through their worldy possessions and in the case of the family's carpenter's business, an accumulation of three generations. I found so much of interest, both facts and photographs relating to those early days, that I began compiling scrap books and have been building up this record ever since.

The reader will be able to see from my collection of photographs relating to Malmesbury that during the latter half of the nineteenth century, many businesses were started, schools opened, and the railway came to the town. It really was a progressive age. In 1875, Malmesbury had 240 commercial business enterprises, including three breweries and 23 public houses.

There are now no breweries, many public houses have closed, and the majority of the old family firms have gone for ever. Not only have the names disappeared from the scene, but often the property has been demolished.

I hope that this book will show that life in 'The Good Old Days' was not 'all work and no play'. Home life had its simple pleasures, the churches were flourishing, and local functions were supported by old and young. Now, we have cars, televisions, computers, and holidays absorbing our time, and organised events often meet a certain amount of apathy. It is very gratifying to know that in the town today we still have the thriving group of Athelstan Players, and a Youth Football Club with 150 members. School children are learning to make Malmesbury Lace and are being given tuition by the Malmesbury Gardening Club.

Although England's oldest borough has extended its boundaries with modern housing estates, I hope future generations will aim to preserve the character of at least the small area of the original hilltop town, still encompassed by its old walls.

Acknowledgements

The author would like to thank the following for permission to use their photographs in this book, and also for the interesting and valuable information they have provided.

Athelstan Museum, Malmesbury; Mrs J. Blanchard; Mr T. Forward; Miss P. Hinwood; Mr O. Pike; Mr J. Strange; and the Wiltshire Library and Museum Service, Trowbridge.

One
History Lesson

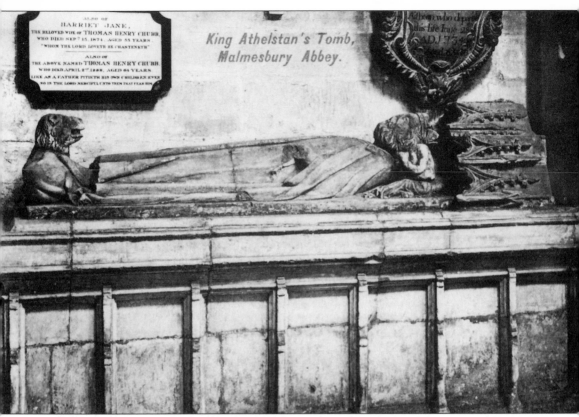

A fourteenth-century effigy of King Athelstan in the north aisle of Malmesbury Abbey. In AD 937 King Athelstan, a grandson of Alfred the Great, granted Kings Heath to the Malmesbury townsmen in return for their help in his wars with the Danes. Today, an applicant to become a commoner must be married, have reached the age of maturity, and be the son or son-in-law of a freeman. He must also live within a radius of one-and-a-half miles measured from the central pinnacle of the Market Cross.

The traditional ceremony at Kings Heath, when a new commoner 'takes up his rights'.

At Malmesbury Common, 1 January 1924. Ambrose Clark, Exton, Box, James Pike. A shallow hole was dug in the turf into which the new commoner placed a silver coin; the following words were then recited by the person carrying out the ceremony – 'Turf and twig I give to thee, as King Athelstan gave to me, a good brother thou shalt be'. The initiator then struck the new commoner across the back with a twig, three times, removed the silver from the hole and made tracks for the slappy (the Royal Oak public house) with the other participants in the ceremony. The Royal Oak closed in 1924.

St. John's Courthouse, where new commoners now take up their rights. The ceremony at the Common has long been discontinued.

SOCIAL & PERSONAL GOSSIP

With time-honoured cere-
mony, the Athelstan sitting of
the 1,000-years-old Malmesbury
Commoners' Court was held at
the St. John's Courthouse on
Tuesday, with the High Steward
(Mr. A. Trevelyan Clark) pre-
siding.

Four applicants were ad-
mitted as young commoners and
paid their fines, and the ancient
ceremony of drawing for their
respective plots of the 500 acres
of ground left the burgesses
of Malmesbury by King Athelstan in recognition of their
assistance in the fight against
the Danes was carried out.

The new commoners are Mr.
F. E. Weeks (in his own right)
and Messrs. A. E. Bowen, G. K.
Fry and C. G. Ponting (in their
wives' rights).

Members of the 1,000-Year-Old Malmesbury Commoners' Court arriving for the Athelstan Session at St. John's Court House on Tuesday.

There are four courts held in the year – Trinity Tuesday, King Athelstan's feast day (the following Tuesday), Michaelmas (29 September) and the last day court at the close of the year.

13

The Capital Burgesses and Assistant Burgesses of Malmesbury seated in order of rank at a meeting in St John's Court about 1930. The Old Corporation or the Warden and Freemen of Malmesbury consists of four grades, rising from a commoner to landholder, assistant burgess (of which there are 24), and finally 12 capital burgesses. There is also a high steward, who in the past was not necessarily a commoner.

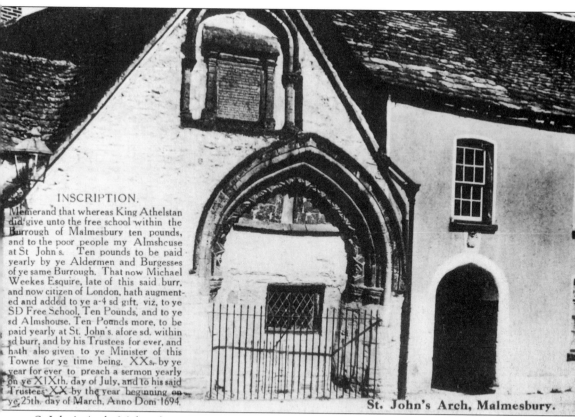

INSCRIPTION.

Mem¢rand that whereas King Athelstan did give unto the free school within the Burrough of Malmesbury ten pounds, and to the poor people my Almshcuse at St John's. Ten pounds to be paid yearly by ye Aldermen and Burgesses of ye same Burrough. That now Michael Weekes Esquire, late of this said burr, and now citizen of London, hath augmented and added to ye a 4 sd gift, viz, to ye SD Free School, Ten Pounds, and to ye sd Almshouse, Ten Pounds more, to be paid yearly at St. John's, afore sd, within sd burr, and by his Trustees for ever, and hath also given to ye Minister of this Towne for ye time being. XXs. by ye year for ever to preach a sermon yearly on ye XIXth. day of July, and to his said Trustees XX by the year beginning on ye 25th. day of March, Anno Dom 1694.

St. John's Arch, Malmesbury.

St John's Arch, Malmesbury.

A detail of the original site.

King Athelstan's Millenary
(A.D. 924 — 1924).

This year marks the 1000th Anniversary of the Accession of King Athelstan, who was crowned at Kingston on Thames and buried in Malmesbury Abbey.

Athelstan was a great benefactor to the Town of Malmesbury: he confirmed the Charter which had been granted by his father Edward the Elder, he conferred various privileges on the Burgesses, and he gave them King's Heath, which still remains in their possession.

The annual ''Athelstan Feast'' will be held on Tuesday, 24th June, and it has been decided to mark the Millenary by a public celebration, which it is hoped will be worthy of so notable an occasion. The suggested programme includes

1. Public Service in the Abbey.
2. Historical Procession.
3. Performances of Historical Play in the grounds of Burton Hill House.
4. Tea for 560 school children.
5. Tableaux by Boy Scouts.
6. Public Dinner in the Town Hall.

The details of these events will be fully advertised.

It is obvious that this celebration will entail considerable expense, which must be raised by subscriptions. May we ask for your kind co-operation and support?

Subscriptions may be paid to Lloyds Bank, Malmesbury, the Midland Bank, Malmesbury, or the Collectors, Mr. S. Bowman, The Suffolk Arms; Mr. E. G. Bartlett, St. Elmo, Sherston Road; and Mr. L. W. Jones, High Street.

JAMES A. JONES,   Mayor.

MONTAGU H. CHUBB, High Steward.

Malmesbury, 7th June, 1924.

Burton Hill House. This was the scene for King Athelstan's Millenary in 1924, which was held here by kind permission of Captain Gordon Miles. This house is now a school for handicapped children. (By kind permission of Captain Gordon Miles)

The Millenary (as detailed opposite) was a memorable occasion and the procession must have been most impressive. It was headed by a company of Saxon warriors and Saxon ladies all on horseback, followed by the commoners attired as their forefathers. King Athelstan was portrayed by Mr F.G. Bartlett and with his courtiers and mace bearers presented a really regal scene. Also in attendance were the Mayor (Councillor J.A. Jones) and corporation, the fire brigade, Buffaloes, Oddfellows, and the Foresters in their picturesque 'Sherwood' dress. The boy scouts and girl guides were there in Saxon garb.

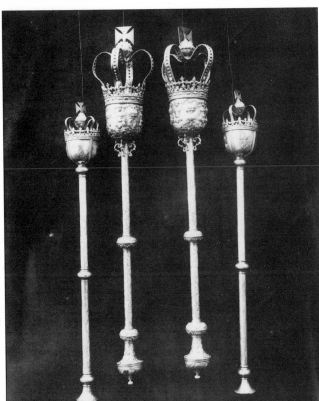

The four beautiful silver gilt ceremonial maces presented to the Old Corporation, two in 1646 and a further pair in 1703.

St John Street decorated for a Coronation street party in June 1953. It shows the almshouses before renovation. They were disused from the 1950s until they were restored in 1968.

1, MARKET CROSS,

MALMESBURY, WILTS.

7th March, 1940.

DEAR SIR/MADAM.

War time cultivation of Malmesbury Common.

For many years past the Trustees of King's Heath have been gravely concerned about the state of cultivation of Malmesbury Common. Various schemes have been inaugurated for grouping together allotments in order to facilitate their better cultivation. By this means an income has been assured to allotment holders, and allotments have been and are still being improved instead of being allowed to fall into a state of dilapidation. *Despite these efforts on the part of the Trustees, the condition of Malmesbury Common is still very far from satisfactory.*

It is now imperative in the National interest that every plot of ground suitable for Corn production should be so employed. The Prime Minister and members of all political parties have made this abundantly clear, and the various County War Agricultural Committees have been empowered to take all necessary steps to ensure maximum production for the duration of the War and for a period of three years thereafter. It is generally admitted that Malmesbury Common, if properly cultivated, would be one of the finest corn-producing tracts of land in the County, and the Trustees are determined to make every effort to help the National Cause in this direction. They hope the desired end can be brought about by voluntary co-operation on the part of all allotment holders, *but if this fails they will not hesitate to invoke the compulsory powers now in force* for ensuring the maximum production of foodstuffs on Malmesbury Common.

The Trustees have now received offers to rent large blocks of allotments for corn production purposes, and they propose to lease such allotments to approved tenants for terms of seven years, so that each allotment holder will receive a *minimum* rent—paid through the Trustees—of Ten shillings per annum throughout the seven years. *Your allotment is amongst the number included in the scheme, and if you agree to the proposal will you please sign, detach and return to me immediately the form of consent set out below?*

In order that there shall be no possible misunderstanding I am instructed to inform you that if you fail to signify your consent to the proposed scheme, you will render yourself liable either

(a) To be discommoned at a special Court to be held immediately for that purpose on the ground that your allotment is not being properly cultivated, or

(b) To be called upon by the County War Agricultural Committee to plough your allotment and cultivate it properly for corn production.

The Trustees hope that every allotment holder concerned will be sufficiently patriotic to consent to the proposed scheme, and thus make a modest contribution to the National cause. By so doing you will help yourself and your country.

It is absolutely imperative that the scheme be put into operation immediately.

By order of the Trustees,

W. TREVELYAN CLARK,

Clerk.

In 1940 King's Heath was taken over by the War Agricultural Committee for war time cultivation. It is now let to tenant farmers with the commoners receiving appropriate remuneration.

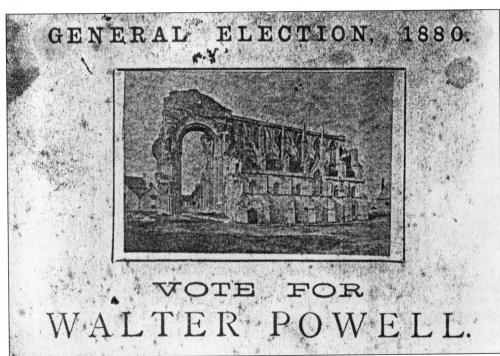

GENERAL ELECTION, 1880.

VOTE FOR
WALTER POWELL.

After a day's excitement the result was announced from a window in the Town Hall – Walter Powell, 607, Albert Kitching, 310. Until the Great Reform Act of 1832, the parliamentary franchise of Malmesbury was restricted to the thirteen Capital Burgesses and like many other 'rotten' boroughs, subject to bribery and corruption.

GENERAL PARLIAMENTARY ELECTION, 1880

MALMESBURY BOROUGH.

MR. ALBERT G. KITCHING

Respectfully solicits the favour of Your

VOTE AND INTEREST

AT THE APPROACHING ELECTION.

Walter Powell, M.P. He was a great benefactor to Malmesbury, building a reading room in Silver Street (now used as a church). He also built a ragged school in Burnivale and supplied fifty tons of coal every winter for the aged poor of the town, as well as tea and sugar.

Sadly Mr Powell disappeared in a hot air balloon at Bridport on 9 December 1881.

A re-enactment of Mr Powell's flight at Bremilham School, Malmesbury, on 31 August 1963.

Two

A Tour of the Town

A picturesque scene of the hill top town from Daniel's Well.

Another view of Malmesbury from Holloway showing the old pumping station (now demolished) in the foreground and, next to the steeple, the old water tower on the sky line. This has since been converted to a private residence, with marvellous panoramic views.

Climbing Holloway Hill, the East Gate approach to the town.

The Guildhall in Oxford Street, owned by the Old Corporation and thought to have been built in 1411. Shown here as a dwelling house, it has since been tastefully restored and is now a restaurant.

Floods at Baskerville on 11 July 1968. To the left, behind the stone wall, is the town bowling green and, in the background, Wynyard Mill.

Another steep approach to the town – Back Hill stone steps rising from Baskerville and leading to Silver Street.

Market day in the Cross Hayes showing Duck and Son brewery to the left of the Town Hall. The brewery was demolished in 1927.

Borough of Malmesbury.

TABLE OF TOLLS

Leviable by the Mayor, Aldermen, and Burgesses of the Borough of Malmesbury, acting by the Council, in the Market provided by such Mayor, Aldermen and Burgesses.

For every Horse, Mare, or Gelding brought into the Market for Sale or exposure for Sale	1s.
For every Entire Horse for Exhibition	1s.
For every Steer, Cow, or Heifer brought into the Market for Sale or exposure for Sale	3d.
For every lot of ten Sheep, Lambs, or Pigs brought into the Market for Sale or exposure for Sale, or any less number exceeding six	9d.
For every lot of six Sheep, Lambs, or Pigs brought into the Market for Sale or exposure for Sale, or any less number	6d.
For every Bull brought into the Market for Sale or exposure for Sale	1s.
For every Calf brought into the Market for Sale or exposure for Sale	3d.
For every Waggon Load or Cart Load of Hay or Straw brought into the Market for Sale or exposure for Sale	1s.
For every Agricultural Implement brought into the Market for Sale or exposure for Sale	1s.
For every Waggon, Cart, Truck, Barrow, or Carriage brought into the Market for Sale or exposure for Sale	1s.
For every Cargo of Timber brought into the Market for Sale or exposure for Sale	5s.

WEIGHBRIDGE TOLLS.

For the Weighing at the Weighbridge in the Market-place of any Waggon	6d.
Of any Cart	3d.
Of any Beast	6d.
Of any Lot of ten Sheep or Pigs or any less number exceeding one	6d.
Of any one Pig or Sheep	3d.

The Seal of the above Council was hereunto affixed and duly attested this twelfth day of September, 1922.

F. WEEKS, Mayor.
M. H. CHUBB, Town Clerk. (L.S.)

Approved by the Minister of Health this thirtieth day of September, 1922.
F. L. TURNER,
Assistant Secretary Ministry of Health. (L.S.)

It cost good money to bring goods or cattle to the market!

Nos 16 and 18 Silver Street. In 1953 the Town Surveyor reported to the Council that in Silver Street 15 people shared one water tap and only three lavatories, which were not of the flush type.

LOT 2.

Two Desirable Stone Built COTTAGES

KNOWN AS

Nos. 16 and 18, Silver Street, Malmesbury.

Together with Gardens

In the respective occupations of Messrs. F. H. Lewis and V. J. Wells at rents amounting in the aggregate to £12 2s. 8d. per annum. Tenant paying rates.

This property formed part of the estate of the late Matthew Thompson for sale by auction at the King's Arms Hotel, Malmesbury, on Wednesday 22 May 1929. Most of the cottages were sold, but these were withdrawn at £70.

A rear view of the same cottages.

Cross Hayes Lane and Tower House in Oxford Street. Tower House was for many years a doctor's residence and surgery. The tower was used as a 'look-out' by the Observer Corps in the last war.

Dr Kinneir in the garden at Tower House, c. 1900.

Market Lane, which has recently been resurfaced. Mercifully, the old mounting steps to the left of the picture remain.

By contrast, the Market Cross and Abbey from the High Street *c.* 1860. Original lithograph by William Hanks (artist and photographer) in the Athelstan Museum, Malmesbury.

Cottages in High Street Hill in 1931. The lower one was always known as the 'Roundhouse' due to its shape. These are near the site of the South Gate to the town, with King's Wall at the rear.

On the opposite side of the street, numbers 74, 76, and 78.

Mrs Elizabeth Barnes clipping the topiary in the garden of 74 High Street in 1972; the old town wall which ran between numbers 72 and 74 can be seen behind the trellis fence.

A view of the Abbey from the north (c. 1913) showing Abbey House on the left. This was built over the cellars of the Abbey buildings and enlarged and modernised in 1580. Later, it was acquired by Captain E.M.S. MacKirdy, who built an extra wing and enclosed the great doveyard with iron railings, and used this area as a kitchen garden. It has since been converted to the very pleasant Cloister Gardens.

The Market Cross with a gas lamp erected in 1836. The building behind was the Cottage Hospital, built in 1897 on the site of the 'Prince and Princess' inn. It is now the Whole Hog restaurant.

The Cottage Hospital from 1897 to 1925.

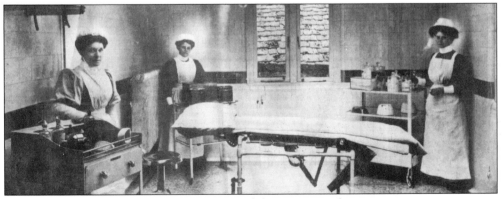

The operating theatre showing three nurses and their antiquated equipment.

X Matthew Hanks was a leading man in Malmesbury a century ago. He was a Capital Burgess. He lived on the Abbey Row, He has been dead many years. I this day asked an aged man — Frank Frie whose years are near 90 if he remembered M.H. He said he did and that he was a very tall fine built man, and that towards the end of his days he suffered from fatness and this interfering with the action of his heart, an operation was performed. His body was opened and he, M.H. held the candle whilst the surgeon removed a portion of fat from near his heart. He survived the operation and lived many years after. His son Joseph Hanks I remember well, as town Surveyor (salary £10 per an) he also was a tall fine man, and like his Father was a burgess. He (J.H) had two sons I remember Jas. Hanks and Mark Hanks — both adherents of the strict Baptist cause of Malmesbury. These two men were of ordinary stature but very honest and straight in their dealings. They have been dead several years.

March 26/80.

A.V. Grimwood.

Probably M.H. died about the year 1815.

A gruesome account in surgery in bygone days.

36

Malmesbury Cottage Hospital on the Chippenham Road in its early days. It has been considerably extended since then, thanks to the supreme efforts of the Friends of Malmesbury Hospital and provides an invaluable service to the town.

The Priory in 1965. It stood next to the Cottage Hospital and was built about 1900 by the stepmother of Montague Chubb. Sadly, it has been demolished. It was occupied for many years by Col. Morrice, who owned Priory Farm on the opposite side of the Swindon Road. In the late afternoon, a Mr Bill Woodward would be sitting in the dairy measuring out rich creamy milk to all who came with their milk cans, which was a pleasant duty for many of us young children after school – no question of being molested or road safety in those days.

Site of the Postern Gate and another steep climb to the town. The three-cornered building at the foot of the steps was at one time used by the Scouts and in the 1940's was taken over by Linolite Ltd as a temporary accounts office after a fire at the Mill Works. The quaint shaped house was occupied by the Misses L. & E. Hanks in their retirement. In 1925, they were still running a toy and newspaper shop in the High Street, where W.H. Smith is today.

The Holy Well of St. Aldhelm at the rear of a house in Abbey Row. Aldhelm became Abbot of the Monastery of Malmesbury in AD 672.

Malmesbury Workhouse.

Malmesbury Union Workhouse on the Bristol Road, built in 1834 and demolished 1971–2. It had a separate hospital building and catered for the destitute and sick. Quite a number of children were there and attended school in their 'workhouse' uniform. The garden was cultivated by permanent inmates and each night tramps paid for their accommodation by breaking up heaps of large stones for metalling the roads before the days of tarmacadem. The workhouse was eventually sold to the Borough Council for £1,800 and converted into flats.

Modern residences on the old workhouse site, 1993. The outline of the Porter's Gate can be seen in the wall.

Seventeenth-century gabled cottages in the Horsefair, Malmesbury.

Three

Public Houses
and Shops

LOT 8.

THE SUBSTANTIALLY BUILT;

Stone Tiled Dwelling House

(Formerly known as The Volunteer Inn) being

No. 133, High Street, Malmesbury.

Together with Garden and Outbuildings.

The House contains 2 Reception Rooms, 4 Bedrooms and the usual domestic offices, now in the occupation of Mr. T. Wheal at an annual rental of £12.

The Purchaser of this lot shall enter into a covenant not to use the premises or any part thereof or any building or erection now or hereafter to be built or erected thereon for the Sale of any Beer, Ale, Porter, Stout, Wines, Spirits, or other Alcoholic Liquors either wholesale or retail for consumption on or off the premises.

170 E. Carter

Particulars and conditions of sale of property by auction at the King's Arms Hotel, Malmesbury, on 22 May 1929. The Volunteer Inn was closed in 1922 and belonged to Matthew Thompson, Mayor of Malmesbury, in 1916, 1917, and 1919. He was a temperance follower and bought up Public Houses in order to close them. There was a provision in the deeds banning the sale of alcohol in the future.

On the outskirts of the town the Black Horse Inn – closed and demolished in 1971 together with the cottage in the foreground, which was occupied for many years by the Wallington family. It has now been replaced by the modern Barley Close flats.

The Bear Inn, High Street, closed in 1963.

A High Street scene at the turn of the century, showing the King's Arms hotel on the left and the George Hotel (now a veterinary surgery) on the right. Note the appalling road surface. Tarmacadam was not introduced until after the First World War. In wet weather the mud was scraped up and carted away and on dry summer days there were water sprinklers to lay the dust.

The King's Arms Hotel with its proprietor Harry Hones standing outside. He was a well-known personality and one of the last of the old type of innkeepers, reputedly wearing a bottle-green coat, red waistcoat and beaver hat.

Harry Jones with Field Marshal Earl Roberts, who lived from 1832 to 1914. He first saw service in the Indian Mutiny, when he won the V.C.

The Tap, Cross Hayes, run by the Garlick family from at least 1850 to 1954.

The cottage at the corner of Oxford Street which was at one time the Three Horseshoes, and adjoined a blacksmith's shop belonging to Mr Walter Harris. The cottage later housed the town's first library, but it was demolished in 1957.

Left: The seventeenth-century Abbey Brewery before restoration in 1990. Right: The White Lion Inn *c*. 1927, with its proprietor, H.W. Abbott, in the doorway. This hostelry was mentioned in the novel *Chippinge* by Stanley Weyman, relating to the time of the rotten boroughs, prior to the Reform Act of 1832. It is now a private residence.

The Bell Hotel, Abbey Row, in 1919, looking very much as it does today. It was built on the site of the former Castle.

The Man WHO CAN'T.

The man who can't **EAT**, can't work, can't sleep, can't think or enjoy his pipe. He looks miserable, feels miserable, makes other folks miserable. Indigestion and dyspepsia are wringing the life out of him. He can't eat for lack of appetite and daren't for fear of indigestion's twinges and pains ; can't work for want of strength and energy derived from well digested food ; can't sleep or think because his blood is poisoned and his brain and nerves are starved, and can't enjoy his pipe for the foul taste which lingers in his mouth and indicates a stomach and a liver all gone wrong. To correct this distressing condition, usually all that is needed is a course of the digestive tonic and liver corrective, Mother Seigel's Syrup. Thirty drops, in a little water after each meal, for a few days, restore tone and vitality to the debilitated organs. Then the weariness and pains of indigestion give place to the vigour and buoyancy of health, pure rich blood renews brain and body tissues, and "good digestion waits on appetite."

With the Compliments of

H. N. RATCLIFFE,
Pharmaceutical Chemist,
High Street, MALMESBURY.

Any sufferers from dyspepsia could resort to Mr Norman Ratcliffe, the High Street chemist who would dole out potions and also dress wounds. National Insurance was not introduced until 1911, and until then a visit to a doctor involved a fee which many could not afford.

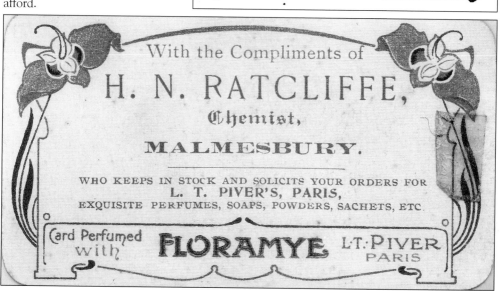

With the Compliments of

H. N. RATCLIFFE,
Chemist,

MALMESBURY.

WHO KEEPS IN STOCK AND SOLICITS YOUR ORDERS FOR
L. T. PIVER'S, PARIS,
EXQUISITE PERFUMES, SOAPS, POWDERS, SACHETS, ETC.

Card Perfumed with FLORAMYE LT·PIVER PARIS

The Three Cups Inn is still a flourishing public house in The Triangle. Also in the Triangle were the Oddfellows Arms, closed in 1922, and the Castle Inn (previously the Weaver's Arms), closed in 1961. Both are now private residences.

The Railway Hotel, built in 1880, changed its name to the Flying Monk when the Station was closed in 1964. The flying monk was Elmer, who attempted a man-powered flight from the top of the Abbey. The Flying Monk sign is now in Malmesbury Museum. The premises were demolished in 1964 to make way for a supermarket.

These premises were built in 1901 and the business finally closed in 1984 when Mr and Mrs David Adye retired. It is now an estate agent.

Choice - -
Mild-Cured
- - Breakfast

Bacon
AND
Hams
(SMOKED AND PLAIN)

Nothing - -
Finer
- Obtainable.

ADYE & SON,
Grocers
AND
Provision
Merchants,
HIGH STREET,
MALMESBURY.

Market Days LAST Wednesday in the Month instead of the Third.

A LARGE SELECTION
OF
FINEST ENGLISH,
Cheddar,
Somerset,
Loaf Cheddar
AND OTHER
Fancy Cheese
ALWAYS IN STOCK.

Adye & Son was established in 1827 and like many old businesses continued through several generations of the same family.

The premises of cycle agent C. Waite being renovated in 1928. This was previously Clements' butchers shop.

The new shop taken over by C.H. White. The premises have recently been further modernised and the business is run by Mr White's son and two grandsons.

An early picture of J.E. Ponting, Ironmonger and Furnishers, in the High Street. These premises later became the town library when it moved from Oxford Street.

The family butcher in 1920 – these premises have since been demolished for road widening.

High Street (3), Malmesbury.

A High Street scene early this century showing Emery's Bakers shop in the foreground, on the right. It later became Tanner's Bakery and this distinctive building was demolished in 1959 and replaced by Barclays Bank. The bakehouse at the back of the premises was in the Cross Hayes and they would willingly bake your Christmas cake for, I believe, a penny, and allow allow one to purchase lovely warm dough, with which my mother made scrumptious lardy cakes. Bread was delivered daily from a handcart, the roundsmen opening your unlocked front door, noting in your 'breadbook' the items he had left, to be paid weekly at the shop. If there was a small child in the home, then occasionally a bread roll like a miniature cottage loaf was left free of charge as a special treat.

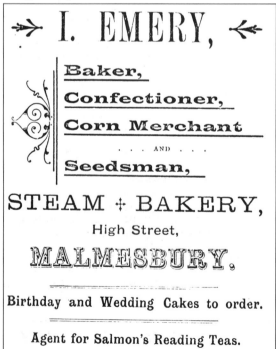

→ I. EMERY, ←

Baker,

Confectioner,

Corn Merchant

. . . AND . . .

Seedsman,

STEAM ✚ BAKERY,

High Street,

MALMESBURY.

Birthday and Wedding Cakes to order.

Agent for Salmon's Reading Teas.

Mr Emery was also a corn merchant and seedsman and the further door and window housed these commodities.

The Milliner, No. 67 High Street – ladies always wore hats in the 'Good Old Days'.

And corsets too!

After the Anstee's sojourn at 61 High Street, the dairy was taken over by the Mortimer family in the early 1900's.

One of the Mortimer daughters with the milk truck and can used for daily deliveries of milk.

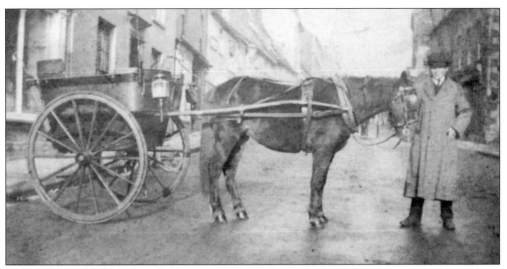
The milk being delivered to the dairy from Marsh Farm, Crudwell Road.

In the early 1920's the dairy business was taken over and run for many years by Mr Frederick Strange. After the last war, his son started a horticultural business in the same premises. Mr Jim Strange seen here shortly before his retirement. It is now a private residence.

Jones and Son, cycle repairers, on 18 December 1913. Charles White, first left, started his own business just before the First World War. This was soon closed when he was on active service, but he started up in business again in the High Street in 1928. Bill Clark from Abbey Mill is second left.

The site of Jones and Son before demolition at the turn of the century.

The new premises built by James A. Jones who was Mayor of Malmesbury in 1911, 1923–24, and 1930–31. As well as cycles, he dealt in motor cars, house furnishing, ironmongery, and music. He drove the first motor car in the town in 1903. The shop is now run by H.J. Knee Ltd.

Frederick Compton, draper, High Street, 1875–95. This is now the Midland Bank.

Riddick's, printers and stationers, at the turn of the century. They ceased trading in 1970.

Another Riddick business in the early days.

Behind the War Memorial, George Woodman's, baker and general store. In the early part of the century he would bake the cottagers home-made bred for a copper or two. The loaves were taken to him in a large clothes basket, suitably covered with a cloth. This is now a private residence.

The Golden Boot in Gloucester Street, this scene dates back to 1878 when the property was purchased by a Mr W. Ball, who was a peddling cobbler. Finding work plentiful in Malmesbury, he eventually achieved his ambition and moved to the High Street where he re-hung his Golden Boot. Also of great interest is the old vicarage next door, with a long window on the ground floor holding some 60 panes of glass. The bay window on the first floor was held up by four carved wooden brackets. The lathe and plaster attic overhung the other two floors. It was demolished soon after this picture was taken and became a stable yard for the adjoining White Lion Inn.

Four

Transport

Old Fire Engine, Malmesbury.

Reputedly the oldest fire engine in England, having been built before the year 1700. It was last used at a fire at Burton Hill House and is now in Malmesbury Museum.

Progress – a more 'modern' version!

The Fire Brigade in the 1920s have now acquired a uniform and helmets.

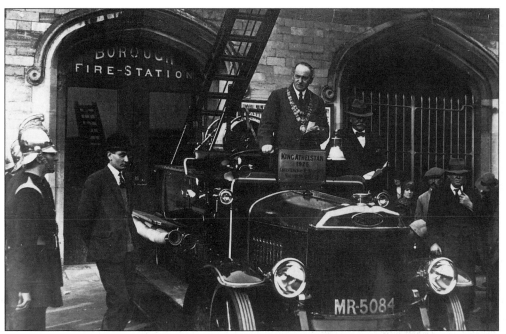

The King Athelstan Fire Engine outside the Fire Station then situated in the Town Hall, Cross Hayes. The Mayor was Captain Scott Mackirdy. The present Fire Station is on the site of the old Railway Station.

The 'Coffee Pot' engine with workers used in the construction of Malmesbury railway line in 1875. The final cost was £87, 094 and 19 shillings. It was opened in 1877 when 300 people went for a free return trip to Dauntsey.

James A. Jones as Mayor of Malmesbury in 1911. He was one of the first passengers on the new railway. He was born in 1868.

Malmesbury Railway Station showing the parcels office, waiting room, booking office, and engine shed. The last trip was to Swindon on 8 September 1951 with only 25 passengers. One of them was again Jimmy Jones!

The railway lines leading from Malmesbury Station and showing the goods shed.

At the goods shed in 1935. Mr Ian Beard, seen here with the first motor lorry. He was sent from Bristol and continued delivering goods until the final closure of the branch in 1962. Mr Ernest Thornbury sadly stands by with the old horse and cart. This service was provided in 1923.

A happy crowd of Malmesbury folk setting forth on a charabanc outing, *c.* 1920.

Jones and Son, Motor Dealers – 'Motor cars for hire – for long or short distances, by the mile, day, week or month'. The speed limit in 1905 was 20 mph.

Outside the Bell Hotel – Fleet of cars now run by E.S.T. Cole of 26 High Street from 1925 – 'Open or closed, cars always on hire to seat 5 or 6 passengers'.

Five

Industry

A typical Malmesbury lacemaker of unknown identity. Lacemaking was a thriving industry in the nineteenth century. According to the 1851 census there were 150 adult lacemakers in the town. By 1881 there were only 11. This decrease was due to the transfer of labour to the Silk Mills, and the old cottage industry virtually died out.

The Avon Silk Mills, originally used for cloth weaving, was in 1852 taken over by Bridget Thomas & Co. and became a silk mill. By 1862 there were 280 workers employed at the mill. It closed in 1941 and our picture shows it as an antique business run by Hugh Dryden. It has since been converted to flats.

The flooded river Avon near the Silk Mills in December, 1965. All the mills in the town were built on the banks of the river, which was controlled by hatches, some being made by Ratcliffe and Son, Westport Ironworks, an old family business still surviving. If the hatches were not raised in wet weather to allow the passage of water, then severe flooding frequently occurred. Most of these hatches have now been replaced with weirs.

Cowbridge House in 1907, home of the de Bertidano family. It was taken over by E.K. Cole Ltd for radar production during the last war.

The entrance to Cowbridge House from the Swindon Road as it looks today.

Fred Barnes at Malmesbury Gasworks in the
1920's. After the introduction of North Sea Gas,
the gasometers were dismantled.

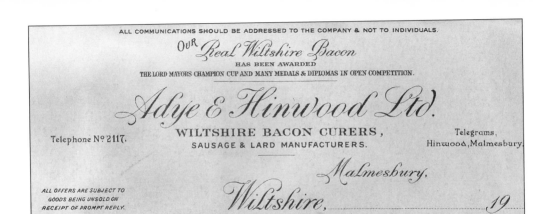

Thomas Lot Hinwood who started Adye and Hinwood Ltd *c.* 1877 seen here with his wife, Mary, and sons Henry Smyth, William Francis, Frederick Louis, George Whitfield and Ernest Theodore, in July 1873.

Mr S. Grey driving pigs into the bacon factory, Park Road, in 1904.

Sides of bacon in the factory.

Thomas Lot Hinwood and Mary in later years. Thomas Lot was Mayor of Malmesbury in 1892.

The last directors of Adye and Hinwood. R.T. Hinwood, A.L. Hinwood, M. Hinwood, Millie Hinwood, L. Spurling, M. Hinwood, G.W. Hinwood, E.A.T. Hinwood, G.H. Spurling. After closure, the factory was demolished and a housing estate, Willow View Close, replaces it.

The premises in the High Street were purchased in 1877 by Henry Barnes, who started the business. Later, two of his sons, Joseph and Edwin, went in to partnership and at the time of closure in 1972 was run by Edward Barnes, son of Joseph.

The entrance to the workshop. Joseph with his son Edward in the background. c. 1920.

Joseph Barnes in his carpenter's workshop, *c.* 1922.

The staff in the early 1920's, outside the timber shed. George Tanner, Edward Barnes, Jack Poulton, and Bill Woodman.

Edward Barnes in the workshop in 1970.

A.W. Beuttell, M.I.E.E., founder of Linolite Ltd. He first thought of producing a line source of light in 1900. He made the reflectors for the first Linolite installation – the outlining of Westminster City Hall for the coronation of King Edward VII.

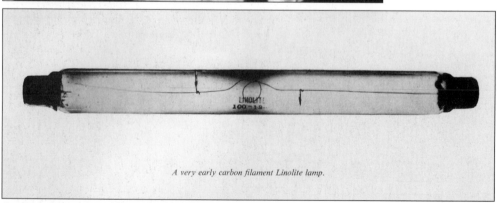

A very early carbon filament Linolite lamp.

A very early carbon filament Linolite lamp. The trade mark 'Linolite' was registered in 1902. The company was situated in the Victoria district of London until their premises were demolished in an air raid in 1941, when it moved to the Mill Works, Malmesbury.

A general view of the Linolite factory at Malmesbury in the early days.

The rear of the factory in 1947 prior to building extensions.

Part of the Linolite factory seen from across the River Avon in 1971. In 1984 Linolite moved to new premises on the Tetbury Road. All the buildings at the Mill Works were demolished and have been replaced by a new housing estate – 'The Maltings'. This name arises from the fact that the building to the right of our picture was originally the malthouse belonging to the brewery started at the end of the nineteenth century by C.R. Luce.

Linolite employees outside the factory in 1947.

The accounts office staff *c.* 1950. Betty Butler, Louie Neal, Brenda Fry, Dorothy Barnes. In the 1940's there was a disastrous fire in the old mill and the accounts office was evacuated to this three-cornered building overlooking the mill works.

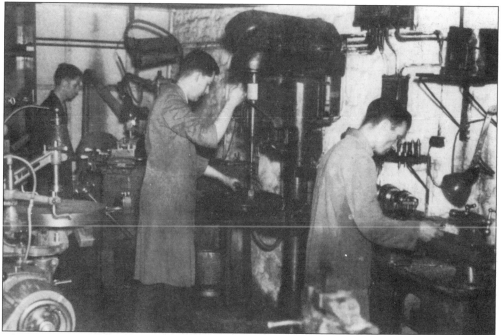

The toolroom in 1947.

The press shop, showing hand and power presses, including a 70-ton press.

A general view of the assembly shop.

In 1984 Linolite moved to new premises on the Tetbury Road. This was closed in 1993, giving rise to much unemployment in the town.

The open-plan offices at the new Linolite premises.

The design office.

Six

Childhood

A delightful study of Arthur Victor Hinwood in his frilly frock. He was born in 1875.

Frederick Henry Barnes in all his finery – much to his disgust in later years!

A group of infants towards the end of the last century. The infants' school was opened on 5 March 1888 and used the upper room at Westport Boys' School. By July 1889 there were 58 children and only one teacher. The five-year-olds were writing capital letters on slates, doing sums, dictation, learning about coins, and some pupils were even taught needlework.

The Infants' school *c.* 1900 with teacher Miss Nella Sharpe. Edward Barnes is fourth from left, back row.

Pupils outside Westport Boys' School.

Another early group – all with their caps on!

Westport Boys' School, *c.* 1902. At centre in the front row is Edward Barnes. Note their stiff white collars!

Westport Boys' *c.* 1930. At the end of the row is teacher Miss Milne, then: (left to right) C. Scott, Ted Paginton, Frank Exton, Jim Mills, Arthur Clark, Jim Strange, Roy Cottell, Wilfred Bick, Eric Woodward, Eddie Fry. Next row, standing: Dick Bowman, Victor Warner, ? Griffiths, John Fraser, George Barnes, Ron Saunders, John Reeves. Seated, front: Victor Wheadon, Joe Guest, Howard Baker, John Walker.

Cross Hayes, Malmesbury, showing the entrance to the school and the Catholic Church at the turn of the century.

Pupils outside Cross Hayes School. The school is now the town library.

Another group at Cross Hayes School towards the end of the last century.

Cross Hayes Infants' School in 1930.

The old Technical School built in 1902, became Malmesbury Secondary School, then the Grammar School, and finally the Church of England Primary School. It was demolished to make way for a new primary school in 1983.

On the front door steps of Malmesbury Secondary School, 25 July, 1939. Back row, Iris Shortall, Marion Stone. Front row: Anita Osmond, Freda Barnes, and Mary Bailey – in their summer uniform of emerald green dresses with white collar and cuffs.

The trim Secondary School winter uniform in 1935. The colours were navy blue and emerald green.

Stainsbridge College, a private girls' school, at the beginning of the century. It then became the residence of retired solicitor Mr F.E. Smith, a National Children's Home, a hotel, and finally a nursing home.

Mary Janes Barnes, the elder daughter of Joseph Barnes. Her mother died of typhoid fever in 1899, which was rampant in the town at the time. As there was no photograph of her, Joseph immediately had pictures taken of all his children.

Sisters Adelaide, Ellen, and Margaret.

Brothers William and Edward Barnes.

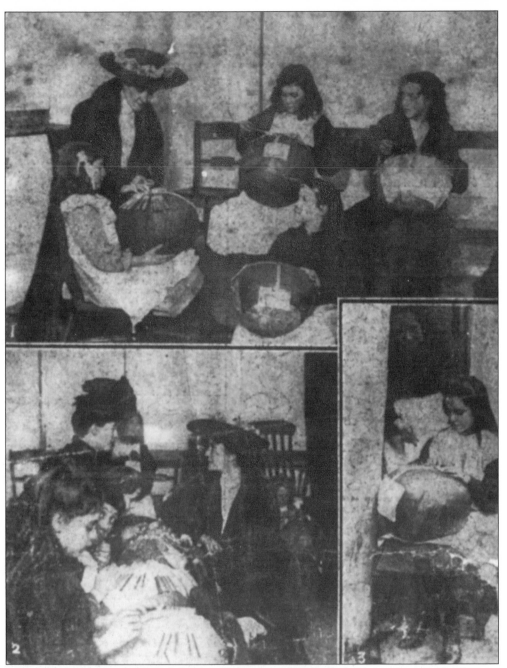

Lady Suffolk became concerned that the old craft of Malmesbury Lacemaking might die out, and in 1907 she organised a lace school which was held in the market room at the King's Arms Hotel, High Street, Malmesbury. Here she is seen visiting the school.

Malmesbury Lacemaking School, c. 1909. From left to right: (back row) Elsie Vaughan, Florrie Bishop, May Jacobs, May Tanner. Middle row: Florrie Weeks, Ms Denley, Mrs Jones (the proprietress of the King's Arms), Miss Fisher (teacher), Florrie Drew, Cassie Drew. Bottom row: Daisy Jefferies, Hilda Fry, Maud Phelps, Nell Jefferies, May Reeves, Eva Jefferies, Kitty Bond.

Now it has passed to the next generation – Mrs Elizabeth Barnes (née White) with her daughter Dorothy, 29 August 1932.

Elizabeth White with her lace.

MALMESBURY AND DISTRICT
Horticultural & Floral Society
Thursday, Aug. 15th, 1912.

FIRST PRIZE
+ Cup.

Miss Lizzie White.

One of the many awards she won for her lace.

Seven

Recreation

The Police Band in the Cross Hayes in 1880.

Queen Victoria's Golden Jubilee
celebrations in the Cross Hayes in
1887.

Shop and May's entry in festive
mood. May's Entry was so called at
the turn of the century and runs
from the High Street to the Cross
Hayes. It is now known as 'The
Gant'.

Crowds celebrating the Diamond Jubilee of Queen Victoria in June 1897. This picture, taken in the Cross Hayes, shows the Town Hall on the right in the background. It was built in 1854 by Fielder and Rich, Auctioneers, as a Sale Room and a letting for concerts, etc. The building to the left was the brewery of Duck and Son, demolished in 1927. Its replacement now forms part of the Civic Centre.

The homecoming of the Earl and Countess of Suffolk after their marriage in 1904. They are seen here at the Market Cross where they were given an address of welcome by the Mayor (Councillor Reed) on 12 January 1905. This was the nineteenth Earl of Suffolk and he was killed in 1917 in Mesopotamia, during the First World War.

Charlton Park, home of the Suffolks, where the Earl and Countess later entertained the tenantry on the estate and many of the inhabitants of Malmesbury on 25 and 26 July, 1905. There were firework displays and music by the Band of the Scots' Guards and Gloucestershire Hussars. The lovely home at Charlton Park is now divided into flats.

Malmesbury Football Club, 1906/7. Standing, left to right: E. Angell (Hon. Sec.), A. Golding, H. Barnes, A. Besant, W. Paginton, D. Pike. Centre row: F. Golding, D. Box, J. Player. Front row: C. Angell, F. Strange (Captain), G. Poole.

Malmesbury Tennis Club, 1911.

A family group after the wedding of a daughter of Edwin Barnes outside their home in Ingram Street, Malmesbury.

Henry Barnes, born on 9 August 1862, died on 11 February 1917. He was an artistic character who played in the Town Band and enjoyed wood carving.

A chair depicting a Shakespearean scene carved by Henry Barnes. It was sold by him when he was short of cash; it is not known who purchased it.

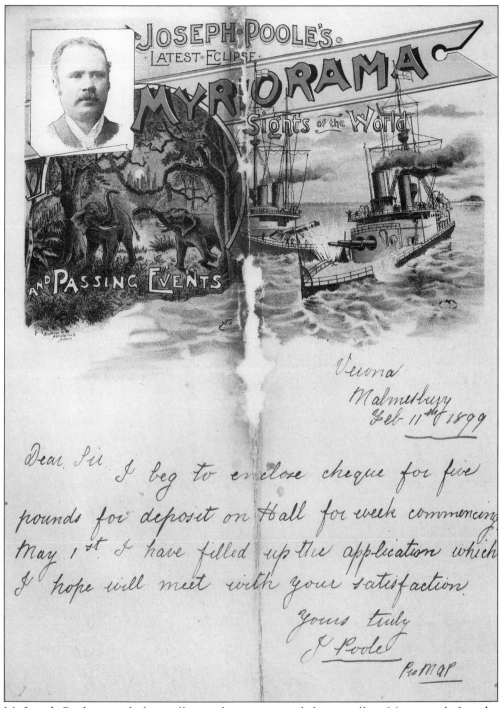

JOSEPH·POOLE'S.
LATEST·ECLIPSE·
MYRORAMA
Sights of the World
AND PASSING EVENTS

Verona
Malmesbury
Feb 11th 1899

Dear Sir,

I beg to enclose cheque for five pounds for deposit on Hall for week commencing May 1st I have filled up the application which I hope will meet with your satisfaction.

Yours truly
J Poole
Pro MaP

Mr Joseph Poole visited places all over the country with his travelling Myrorama before the advent of the moving picture. He was based at Verona House, Malmesbury, and used an adjoining building for painting the Myrorama pictures which were done by an Italian artist. They were shown to the audience through the medium of mirrors accompanied with a dramatic description by a narrator.

Watching the chickens in 1926 on the site of the first cinema in Malmesbury.

The Lincoln Imp Engine used to operate Malmesbury Cinema in the High Street, in 1927. The engineers were Mr George Vanstone and Mr Dick Bishop.

The front of the cinema in 1932, by which time it had 'gone electric'.

The same site in January 1963. The old cinema had been replaced by a Telephone Exchange built in about 1938, but remained unused until after the war. The exchange was then at the Post Office and manned by operators.

The Athelstan Cinema, Market Cross, Malmesbury, built in 1935 and demolished in 1993.

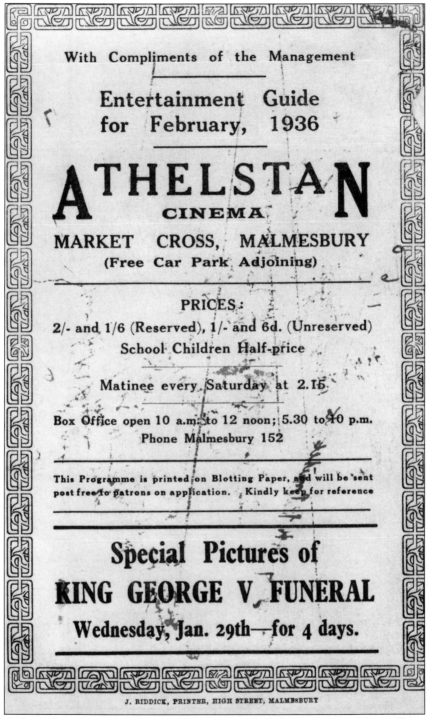

With Compliments of the Management

Entertainment Guide for February, 1936

ATHELSTAN
CINEMA

MARKET CROSS, MALMESBURY
(Free Car Park Adjoining)

PRICES:

2/- and 1/6 (Reserved), 1/- and 6d. (Unreserved)
School Children Half-price

Matinee every Saturday at 2.15

Box Office open 10 a.m. to 12 noon; 5.30 to 10 p.m.
Phone Malmesbury 152

This Programme is printed on Blotting Paper, and will be sent post free to patrons on application. Kindly keep for reference

Special Pictures of
KING GEORGE V FUNERAL
Wednesday, Jan. 29th—for 4 days.

J. RIDDICK, PRINTER, HIGH STREET, MALMESBURY

In days before television, news of national events reached the attention of the public in other ways. In 1918 a war cinema van visited Malmesbury and 'pitched in the Cross Hayes. As darkness fell, hundreds listened to a lecture about the war and a fervent appeal to help the country. At about 9.00pm, vivid war pictures were portrayed on a huge screen.

A day at the seaside used to be a real 'event'. Jim Strange seen here, complete with buckets and spades and Grannie (Mrs Joseph Strange), c. 1926.

Bostock and Wombells circus leaves the town on 5 May, 1931. Note the cinema advertisements in the background.

The Market was held in the Cross Hayes on the last Wednesday in the month. Although important to the local farmers, it was quite a social event for Malmesbury folk. Seen here are Mr Fred Strange, second from left, with his father, Mr Joseph Strange, to the right.

Another happy group watching the proceedings, c. 1930. From left to right: John Paginton (the boy in the cap), Mr Eric Chubb, Mr Mark Poulton (in the white coat), Jim Strange (in the sou'wester), his father, Mr Fred Strange, and Mr Fred Day. The ladies also appreciated the market days when there were trade stalls around the perimeter with a variety of commodities all at bargain prices!

Malmesbury Carnival, 1933 – The Shows in the Cross Hayes.

Malmesbury Carnival, 19 August 1939. We watch the Carnival Queen, Gwen Duke, and her two small attendants in the flower-bedecked carriage at the head of the procession. Note that the cinema has now been superceded by the telephone exchange.

Pupils of music teacher Miss Evelyn Sharpe ALCM in a one-act comedy play at one of her concerts in the YMCA hall. From left to right: Jose Hayes, Phyllis Pike, Jean Wicks, Margaret Law, Dorothy Barnes.

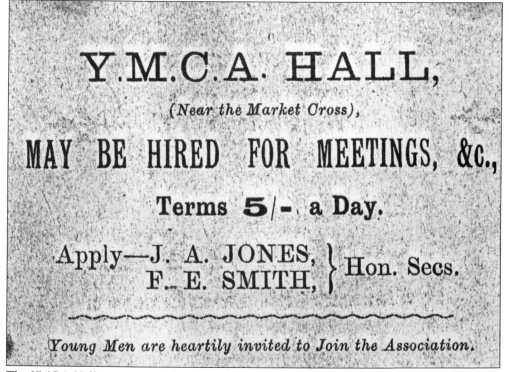

Y.M.C.A. HALL,

(Near the Market Cross),

MAY BE HIRED FOR MEETINGS, &c.,

Terms 5/- a Day.

Apply—J. A. JONES,
F. E. SMITH, } Hon. Secs.

Young Men are heartily invited to Join the Association.

The YMCA Hall, now part of the Civic Centre, was originally built as a Wesleyan church. It could be hired for a more modest fee than the Town Hall.

Saturday afternoon recreation in 1932 – father cuts the lawn!

Mrs Elizabeth Barnes with her topiary in the same garden in 1972.

Eight

Places of Worship

Malmesbury Cross and Abbey. — This beautiful and interesting Cross stands on the site of the histor Cross where it is said that St Aldhelm, finding himself unable to attract the people inside their beautif Abbey used to sit in disguise with his harp, and there preach to the people by means of music and sor

Malmesbury Cross and Abbey. Also note the steeple to the left. This was once attached to the parish church of St. Paul's, the remains of which were taken down in 1852.

Malmesbury Abbey – the ruins, West End.

A much later picture of the West End. The cannon in the foreground is said to have been taken at Sebastopol.

The Abbey, floodlit, in 1951. This shows the West End tastefully restored.

The visit of Queen Mary to Malmesbury Abbey in August 1922.

Malmesbury Abbey interior looking west – note the old pews and the 212-year-old organ with choir stalls either side.

Malmesbury Abbey interior looking east after restoration in 1928. The old pews have been replaced with slatted wooden chairs. The new choir stalls are now in front of the altar.

123

The Triangle, Malmesbury, showing St. Mary's Church in the background. This used to be affiliated with the Abbey, the curate taking many of the services. It is now a community hall. To the left is the War Memorial listing seventy-five names of Malmesbury men who paid the supreme sacrifice in the First World War.

The Triangle in bygone years.

124

The Methodist Church in the Triangle, built in 1899 on the site of three cottages.

An early picture of the interior of St. Aldhelm's Roman Catholic Church, built in 1872, in the Cross Hayes, Malmesbury.

Abbey Row Baptist Chapel, built in 1802 and extended to seat 400 in 1816. Further modernisation took place during the early part of this century. The cottage on the left has long been demolished and the gas lamp over the gate removed. The chapel is now closed.

The interior of the Baptist Chapel before restoration.

An Abbey Row Baptist Sunday School outing to Charlton Park c. 1905. In later years there was a special excursion train to either Weston-super-Mare or Barry Island. All denominations participated and on these days the town was virtually deserted.

Another Baptist gathering at 'The Cliff', 1 July 1926. This was the home of the pastor, Mr Seymour Farmer.

The last open air baptisms in the river behind Abbey House in the early 1900s. According to William of Malmesbury, this was the traditional spot for penance by Aldhelm, Abbot of the Monastery of Malmesbury, AD 672, 'That he might reduce the force of his rebellious body he used to immerse himself up to the shoulders in a spring near the monastery. There, caring neither for the frosty rigor of winter nor the mists rising from the marshy ground in summer, he used to pass the night unharmed.'